Major Competitive Reality Shows:
American Idol

Emma Kowalski

Mason Crest Publishers
Philadelphia

Mason Crest Publishers
370 Reed Road
Broomall, PA 19008
www.masoncrest.com

CPSIA Compliance Information: Batch #060110-MCRS. For further
information, contact Mason Crest Publishers at 1-866-MCP-Book

First printing
1 3 5 7 9 8 6 4 2

Library of Congress Cataloging-in-Publication Data

Applied for
ISBN: 978-1-4222-1668-2 (hc)
      978-1-4222-1931-7 (pb)

Photo credits: AP/Wide World Photo: 4; Getty Images: cover, 34; Mario Anzuoni/Reuters/
Landov: 7; courtesy 19 Entertainment: 12; Fox Broadcasting/Photofest: 10; used under
license from Shutterstock, Inc.: 1, 8, 14, 17, 18, 24, 26, 27, 28, 32, 37, 39, 42; U.S.
Department of Defense: 31; courtesy Yodel Anecdotal (http://www.flickr.com/photos/
yodelanecdotal/4012939906): 13.

Contents

1

A New Champion, A Departing Judge

On Wednesday, May 26, 2010, thousands of people were seated in Nokia Theatre in downtown Los Angeles. An estimated 24.2 million more were watching from home, their televisions tuned to the Fox network. The ninth season finale of *American Idol*, the phenomenally popular competitive reality show, was underway. During this broadcast, the latest champion's identity would be revealed.

The night before, viewers had four hours to decide between the remaining two contestants and cast votes—via phone calls or text messages—for the one they preferred. Now, votes had been counted. The singer who'd earned the most votes would get a record deal and a huge publicity push for his or her major-label debut album. There didn't seem to be an obvious front-runner; when the entire season's votes were counted, there was only a 2 percent difference between the two finalists' tallies. Either Lee DeWyze or Crystal Bowersox would be named the ninth winner of *American Idol*—but not until the end of the finale.

The finalists were new to the spotlight, but had been developing as musicians for much longer. They both wrote songs and could play

multiple instruments. A native of suburban Chicago, Lee worked at a paint store and fronted a garage band. Although he hoped to channel contemporary artists like Sufjan Stevens and Kings of Leon, he also cited older, acoustic guitar-driven acts like Cat Stevens and Simon & Garfunkel as major influences. Crystal performed in churches and as a *busker* around Toledo, Ohio, where she lived with her young son. She had a heavily folk-influenced sound, and enjoyed gritty-voiced rockers like Melissa Etheridge, Ray LaMontagne, and Janis Joplin.

Out of thousands of auditioners, Crystal and Lee were among the few to reach the show's semifinal rounds in January. Since February, they'd performed once a week, and by March, they'd landed in the finals along with ten other singers. The judges—Randy Jackson, Simon Cowell, Kara DioGuardi, and Ellen DeGeneres—weighed in on each performance, but they didn't get to decide who would advance beyond the top 12. Only viewers could determine the contestants' future in the competition, by casting their votes. Each week, the contestant who'd received the lowest number of votes went home. By outlasting so many other singers, both Lee and Crystal had proven themselves as promising young talents who could attract many fans. But only one of them could win.

SAYING GOOD-BYE

This season finale wasn't just dedicated to naming a new champion. It was also a sendoff for Simon Cowell, a creator of *American Idol* as well as

Fans watch as celebrities arrive at the season finale of *American Idol*'s ninth season, May 2010. Many people were sorry to see longtime *Idol* judge Simon Cowell leave the show at the end of the ninth season.

one of its judges. He was leaving to launch a new show called *The X Factor*. Like *American Idol*, it would be an American version of a program launched by Simon in the United Kingdom. It was slated to premiere on Fox in fall 2011. As the judge who was notoriously difficult to impress, Simon was one of the best-known personalities to emerge from *American Idol*.

Throughout the show, Simon's contributions to *American Idol* were discussed. Comedians Ricky Gervais and Dane Cook quipped about Simon's rude reputation. Paula Abdul, who had been a judge from seasons 1 through 8, showed up to crack a few jokes, reminisce, and wish Simon luck. Video *montages* reminded viewers of Simon's harshest critiques. All but one past winner took the stage and sang a song dedicated to Simon (Season 7's David Cook was at a charity fundraiser). Simon wasn't exactly known for his sensitivity, but he seemed touched. "I didn't think I was going to be this emotional," he admitted to the audience, "and I genuinely am."

AMERICA'S NEWEST IDOL

When nearly two hours had passed, it was time to put an end to the suspense and announce the results. Looking rather nervous, the two finalists stood at the center of the stage, joined by the show's host, Ryan Seacrest. The chairman of Telescope, the telecommunications company in charge of collecting and verifying the votes, gave Ryan a silver and gold envelope containing the vote tallies. Crystal put her head on Lee's shoulder as they waited for Ryan to read the name of the winner.

After a few dramatic pauses to build even more tension, Ryan announced that voters had chosen Lee. A stunned-looking Lee thanked his supporters, gave Crystal a hug and some kind words, and talked to the judges and other finalists as they came onstage to congratulate him. When Ryan asked him how he felt about winning, Lee said his feelings were indescribable. As the final credits rolled and Ryan announced the ending of yet another season of *American Idol*, Lee sang through a cascade of confetti.

Just appearing on *American Idol* can help a young singer become a star. Since finishing sixth on the show, Kellie Pickler has become a popular and award-winning country music star.

MOVING FORWARD

Lee DeWyze had a lot to look for-ward to in his year as the *incumbent* champion, but the contestants he'd defeated would also be busy. The top 10 finalists would begin a nationwide tour together on July 1. Each singer would perform a few solo songs, as well as participate in duets and group numbers. 19 Entertainment, the production company behind *American Idol* (along with Fremantle Media), was contractually enti-tled to sign any former contestants who seemed likely to be moneymakers.

Fast Fact

Many *American Idol* contestants are songwriters, but Crystal Bowersox was the first whose original compo-sition was heard on the show. A song she wrote played during an episode when the final three con-testants visited their hometowns.

Within a week of the finale, Lee and Crystal both signed record deals. They also released their first singles, which were covers they'd performed on the show. Lee's debut was a rendition of "Beautiful Day," originally by U2, and Crystal released her version of "Up to the Mountain," written by Patty Griffin. Both singles landed in the top 10 most downloaded songs on iTunes.

As the Season 9 singers forged ahead with their fledgling careers, the *American Idol* production team was also in for an interesting time. It wasn't known who—if anyone—would replace Simon, or how else his departure would change the show. The network also had other con-cerns. Although *American Idol* was still the most-watched show on prime time television, ratings had been declining for a couple of years. Network executives pointed out that this was typical for older shows. Still, many viewers and critics seemed to think the *Idol* formula was growing tired and had run its course. But then, *American Idol* had a long track record of surprising people.

2

The Judges

An important reason behind *American Idol*'s ongoing appeal is its panel of judges. Each judge came to the panel with a different perspective on music and a different attitude toward the competition. Their discussions and critiques are in equal parts informative and entertaining.

SIMON COWELL

In 1963, the Beatles topped the charts with the breakthrough single "She Loves You." As the decade went on, the band would revolutionize popular music. Simon Philip Cowell, born in 1959 in Brighton, England, was among the young people who idolized the Beatles. But unlike most young listeners, Simon was more interested in the band's image and marketing. He would grow up to be an expert in selling music.

Simon's first foray into the recording industry came when his father helped him get a mail room job at EMI Music. In the 1980s, he left EMI to pursue his own projects, ending up at the indie label Fanfare Records. Simon helped Sinitta Malone, his then-girlfriend, launch

Fast Fact

The artists and repertoire (A&R) division of a record label seeks out promising acts to sign to the label. When the artist is signed, the A&R department helps to line up producers and choose singles for the artist's album.

some hit singles in the U.K. When Fanfare's parent company folded, Simon had to move back in with his parents. But Simon soon resumed his plans.

As an A&R consultant at BMG Records, Simon planned innovative moneymaking schemes. Executives were skeptical of his idea to release *novelty* CDs about TV characters (such as the Teletubbies and World Wrestling Foundation personalities), but these soundtracks made money. Simon also found success launching pop acts, including the boy band Westlife and the opera-pop group Il Divo. In 2002, he set up another label, Syco, which later partnered with Sony Music Entertainment. As he developed new television franchises, he signed many of their contestants to Syco.

Simon's first collaboration with Simon Fuller, another extremely successful pop hitmaker, was the creation of *Pop Idol*, the British singing competition that was the basis for *American Idol*. After two seasons, Simon created *The X Factor* as a replacement for *Pop Idol*. In 2007, Simon launched *Britain's Got Talent,*

The British talent manager Simon Fuller created *Pop Idol* and its American spin-off, *American Idol*, as well as many other successful shows.

a reality competition open to all ages and all skills. These shows, both of which featured Simon as the most outspoken judge, also spawned international adaptations. Leona Lewis, who won *The X Factor*'s third season, saw her single "Bleeding Love" hit #1 in 34 countries. Another runaway success was Susan Boyle, the second-place finisher on *Britain's Got Talent* in 2009. Her debut album was the global top seller of that year.

In early 2010, Simon announced his engagement to Mezhgan Hussainy, the head makeup artist for *American Idol*. When he isn't taping in America, he lives in London.

RANDY JACKSON

Born in 1956 in Baton Rouge, Louisiana, Randall Darius Jackson took up the bass guitar when he was 13. Randy honed his talent in college, playing bass on two albums by acclaimed jazz fusion drummer Billy Cobham. This was the first of Randy's many gigs as a session musician—an instrumentalist who accompanies many different acts onstage or in the recording studio. His studio credits include work with Bon Jovi, Bruce Springsteen, and Billy Joel. In 1983, Randy toured with the rock band Journey. He has also performed in

Since *American Idol* made Randy well-known to the general public, he has been involved with other projects. He is the creator and producer of *America's Best Dance Crew*, a group dance competition that premiered in 2008 on MTV. Also in 2008, Randy produced a compilation album called *Randy Jackson's Music Club*. It featured many musicians, including some former *American Idol* contestants.

backing bands for Mariah Carey, Keith Richards, and Aretha Franklin, among many others.

Randy is not only one of the recording industry's most reliable bass players. He has more than two decades of experience as a producer and talent scout. Prior to joining *American Idol*, Randy served as A&R vice president at Columbia Records for eight years and at MCA Records for four. In total, he has worked on over 1,000 albums.

A father of three, Randy has been married to former dancer Erika Riker since 1995. Randy is active in movements to prevent health

Ryan Seacrest

Born in 1974, Ryan John Seacrest grew up outside Atlanta. Thanks to a high school internship at an area radio station, he got an early start in broadcasting. For years, Ryan took small radio and hosting gigs. When he began hosting *American Idol* in 2002, his media career took off.

Ryan's high-profile media work isn't limited to *American Idol*. In 2004, Ryan succeeded well-known broadcaster Casey Kasem as host of the radio show *American Top 40*. His own radio show, *On Air with Ryan Seacrest*, debuted the same year. Based in Los Angeles, the program is syndicated on 150 radio stations. In 2005, Ryan became executive producer of *New Year's Rockin' Eve*, the variety program aired every New Year's Eve on ABC. He also began appearing as co-host alongside the special's longtime host, Dick Clark. Ryan regularly appears on the E! cable network, hosting news segments and red carpet specials.

Ryan is also involved in projects in which he doesn't appear on camera. His self-titled production company is responsible for several reality shows, including *Keeping Up with the Kardashians*, *Bromance*, and *Denise Richards: It's Complicated*. He also owns several restaurants.

problems in young people, such as juvenile diabetes and obesity; he also lends his support to pet adoption centers.

PAULA ABDUL

Born in 1962 in Los Angeles, Paula Julie Abdul developed an interest in dance at a very young age, watching movie-musicals with her parents. Throughout childhood and young adulthood, Paula showed a natural aptitude for dancing and worked hard to improve. During her freshman year of college, Paula tried out for the dance team that performs at Los Angeles Lakers basketball games. She was one of twelve young women to make the team. Within a few months, she became the team *choreographer*. Family members of Janet Jackson admired Paula's work with the Lakers dance team, and hired her to choreograph the rising star's videos.

Working with the Jackson family helped make Paula an in-demand choreographer. Her routines appeared in music videos, television shows, awards ceremonies, and movies, winning her two Emmy Awards and a Grammy Award. Paula began to sing professionally in 1987. Her debut album, *Forever Your Girl*, sold more than 7 million copies.

By the mid-1990s, however, Paula's music career was in decline. She faced personal setbacks as well, including two unsuccessful marriages, chronic pain caused by injuries, and a serious health problem: *bulimia*. Paula took a break from show business to recover. She became a spokesperson for the National Eating Disorders Association, a nonprofit organization that aims to help people affected by eating disorders, and has remained active in eating disorder prevention. By the early 21st century, Paula believed she had overcome her problems and was ready to return to the spotlight. *American Idol* gave her the opportunity to do so.

Paula left *American Idol* over a salary dispute in 2009, but it wasn't very long before she would return to reality television. In May 2010, she was named a judge and executive producer for a dance competition called *Got to Dance,* to be aired on CBS. Paula's other recent activities include fundraising for environmental protection groups and selling her own jewelry line.

KARA DIOGUARDI

Kara Elizabeth DioGuardi was born in 1970 in Westchester County, New York. When she first pursued a career in music, Kara hoped to be a singer. She studied opera at Duke University, and worked for the music magazine *Billboard* after college. However, after some experience with the unforgiving music industry, Kara slowly realized she preferred working behind the scenes. By the early 21st century, Kara was an extremely busy and in-demand songwriter.

Today, Kara's name appears in the songwriting credits of over 120 albums, which have sold a combined total of over 150 million copies. She says the key to a successful career was her genre **versatility**. "If rock was in style, I would do rock songs," she told the *New York Times* in 2009. "If R&B was kicking, I would do R&B." In the early 21st century, Kara wrote or co-wrote a string of hits for female pop singers like Pink, Ashlee Simpson, Britney Spears, Hilary Duff, and Christina Aguilera.

Even before she became a judge, Kara had connections to *American Idol.* She and Paula Abdul collaborated on "Spinning Around," a song that became a big hit for Kylie Minogue in 2000. Kara also wrote songs for several early *Idol* alums. Prior to joining the *American Idol* panel, Kara was briefly a judge on *The One: Making a Music Star*, a singing competition that was cancelled after two weeks in 2006. Coincidentally, Syesha

The panel of *American Idol* judges expanded to four in 2009, when songwriter Kara DioGuardi joined the team for the show's eighth season.

Mercado, a contestant on *The One*, finished in third place on *American Idol* in Season 7.

Kara divides her time between Los Angeles and coastal Maine. In 2009, she married contractor Michael McCuddy. Her charitable efforts include work with drug rehabilitation centers and animal welfare groups.

ELLEN DEGENERES

Actress, television personality, and stand-up comedian Ellen DeGeneres was born in 1958 near New Orleans. Her career in entertainment began in the early 1980s, when she performed stand-up comedy regionally and then nationally. Later, she began taking small parts on television and in movies. She starred in the hit sitcom *Ellen* from 1994–1998, and a second, unrelated sitcom called *The Ellen Show* from 2001–2002. In 2003, Ellen provided the voice of a forgetful fish in the animated movie *Finding Nemo.*

In her hit stand-up specials, Ellen told jokes that were witty and observational, without resorting to profanity or personal insults. This playful style of humor lends itself well to high-profile events. She hosted the Academy Awards in 2007, and has hosted the Emmy Awards

Ellen DeGeneres is on stage with the Jonas Brothers while taping her daytime talk show in Orlando. Ellen often spoke about how much she enjoyed watching *American Idol*. She joined the panel of *Idol* judges for Season 9.

three times. Ellen also brought her comic flair to her daytime talk show, *The Ellen DeGeneres Show,* which premiered in 2003. In its first year alone, the show was nominated for 12 Emmy Awards.

When Ellen was named the newest addition to the *American Idol* judges' panel in September 2009, some of the show's fans were puzzled at the choice of someone without direct involvement in the music industry. Executive producer Cecile Frot-Coutaz explained the decision. "Ellen knows what it takes to create a connection with the audience. The show is not just about being able to sing. It is about the ability to create a connection and getting people to fall in love with you."

In July 2010, Ellen announced that she would not return for the show's 10th season. "I . . . realized this season that while I love discovering, supporting and nurturing young talent, it was hard for me to judge people and sometimes hurt their feelings," she explained. "I loved the experience working on 'Idol' and I am very grateful for the year I had. I am a huge fan of the show and will continue to be."

3

Persistence Pays Off

In early 2001, Simon Cowell and Simon Fuller traveled to the United States to pitch their idea for a televised singing competition. Viewers would choose the winner, who would receive a record deal. Back in the United Kingdom, they had no trouble selling this idea, which was being developed into a show called *Pop Idol.* It would premiere that October, featuring Cowell as a judge. Simon Cowell felt confident that an American network would also be interested in the format.

However, no network responded to the pitch. Other music competitions had aired before, and they tended to be minor hits at best. Many American television executives now believed that reality TV and music didn't mix.

These rejections were rough, but *Pop Idol* proved extremely successful. Months after their original pitch, the Simons got an offer from an American network that had already turned them down. Rupert Murdoch, the founder of the Fox network, found out about *Pop Idol* from his daughter, who was a big fan. He insisted that the network pick up the American adaptation, and forbade the production team from changing the format more than necessary. The new show came to be called *American Idol*, and was set to premiere on June 11, 2002. That premiere would attract an astonishing 10 million viewers.

THE ORIGINAL JUDGES' PANEL

Simon Cowell didn't expect to play an on-camera role on *American Idol*. He certainly was a memorable personality on *Pop Idol*, but he assumed that an American show would only hire American judges. Besides, he was under the impression that his harshness was less socially acceptable in the United States. As it turned out, the Fox team enjoyed his **persona** on *Pop Idol* and wanted to bring him on board. Simon accepted the position only after producers reassured him that he wouldn't have to tone down his act.

Along with two hosts, Ryan Seacrest and Brian Dunkleman, two more judges were recruited: Randy Jackson and Paula Abdul. The three judges didn't have much time to get acquainted before the cameras started rolling. Auditions began in the spring of 2002, in seven American cities.

When she realized how tough Simon was going to be on the less-talented auditioners, Paula grew upset and nearly quit the show. Although Simon intervened to help convince her to stay, the two didn't get along very well for a while. However, Simon and Paula eventually became close friends, and the judges' tense on-air disagreements evolved into fun banter. "He's like the brother I never had," Paula quipped about Simon to *Ladies' Home Journal*, "or wanted."

Viewers quickly came to expect the judges' critiques to follow an established pattern. Paula tried to say at least one nice thing about every performance, while Simon told people exactly what he thought about their singing. Randy tended to fall somewhere in between, offering constructive criticism to contestants while trying not to make them feel bad about themselves.

THE SEASONAL FORMAT

American Idol's first season established the pattern that would make the show an ongoing smash. The first episodes show the judges looking for talent in different American cities. Open tryouts are held in stadiums. Contestants who get past preliminary screenings must sing *a cappella* in front of the judges. Each judge votes whether or not to pass a contestant to the next round. If the contestant is accepted, he or she gets a ticket to Hollywood.

When all the cities have been visited, semifinal rounds begin in Hollywood. The semifinalists are narrowed down from hundreds to a

Changes to the Show

When the Fox network picked up the show that became *American Idol*, the plan was to change as little as possible from the succesful *Pop Idol* format. However, certain minor changes were necessary for the show to work in the United States.

One difference between the shows is that *American Idol* is aired twice a week, while *Pop Idol* was only aired weekly. This is because all of Great Britain is in the same time zone, while the United States spans several time zones. Placing the results show on a separate night makes voting equally convenient for all American viewers.

The reason the American adaptation's title was changed from *Pop Idol* to *American Idol* was that the word "pop" had a different connotation in American slang. It referred to a specific genre of radio-friendly music, as opposed to the wide-reaching musical appeal the production team hoped the show would have. In the British music industry, the term "pop" was more broad.

few dozen. Ultimately, the best of the semifinalists are passed to the final round. On Season 1, the final round began when just ten contestants were left. (In later seasons, this number increased slightly.)

PERFORMANCES AND RESULTS

During the final rounds, Tuesday nights are dedicated to the contestants' performances. Early in the season, contestants sing one song each, but in later weeks, they sing two. The contestants choose songs from a list that usually revolves around a theme. The night could be devoted to a single genre, such Motown or disco. All songs might be from the catalogue of a single artist, like Elvis Presley or the Beatles. Each contestant might have to choose a song that was released the year he or she was born. Some theme nights are relatively flexible and allow the contestants some freedom to choose what genres they want to sing, such as "Songs from the Cinema." When a contestant finishes singing, he or she listens to the judges' critiques. Then, toll-free phone numbers are displayed. Viewers who liked the contestant's performance call or text these numbers to cast votes.

On Wednesday, the contestants, judges, and viewers find out who received the most votes and who will be going home. The results episodes are shorter than the performance episodes. They usually get started with a group musical number, such as a *medley* of songs relating to the week's theme. If a guest judge or mentor played a role this week, he or she might also

Fast Fact

American Idol's biggest corporate sponsors are Coca-Cola, Ford, and AT&T. By 2008, the companies paid $35 million per season to air commercials during each episode, and to have their logos placed around the set.

perform. At the end of the episode, the singer with the lowest vote count is revealed. That contestant performs one last time before leaving the set. A montage of the contestant's time on the show plays. Each season has a different song accompanying these montages.

FIGHT TO THE FINISH

Week after week, singers are eliminated until only two remain. On the last Tuesday episode of the season, each finalist performs three songs. Usually, the finalist selected one of his or her songs, a judge chose another, and a record executive (such as Simon Fuller) chose

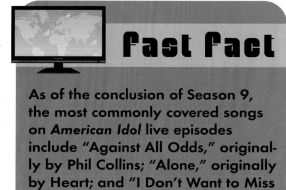

Fast Fact

As of the conclusion of Season 9, the most commonly covered songs on *American Idol* live episodes include "Against All Odds," originally by Phil Collins; "Alone," originally by Heart; and "I Don't Want to Miss a Thing," originally by Aerosmith.

the third. The season finale will take place the next night, and Tuesday's biggest vote-getter will be named the *American Idol* champion.

During the season finale, all the finalists return to sing, backed by famous musicians. As the season's memorable moments are discussed, the mood is festive but suspenseful. At the end of the finale, the winner is named. The new winner performs what will be his or her debut single. These tunes generally have uplifting lyrics; fans playfully call them "coronation songs." Usually, they are composed specifically for the show, but on at least two occasions, they have been covers.

THE FIRST IDOL

As Season 1 continued, Simon realized that he couldn't always predict how the voters would feel. He wouldn't always agree with the results, either. He declared early on that Tamyra Gray was his favorite contestant

Kelly Clarkson proved that *American Idol* winners really could go on to successful careers in the music industry. Kelly's first four albums sold more than 10 million copies in the United States. She has also recorded many hit singles since winning the first *Idol* competition in 2002.

of Season 1. In the weeks before the season finale, he assumed the top two would be Tamyra and Kelly Clarkson. He was right about Kelly, but to his surprise, Tamyra finished fourth. Instead, Kelly's competition in the Season 1 finale was Justin Guarini. Kelly was named the winner of Season 1 on September 4, 2002, in front of 22.8 million viewers.

The fanfare that greeted Kelly exemplified the advantages of *American Idol* as an introduction to a new artist. Viewers knew she wasn't *lip-synching* onstage. Compared to pop stars whose public images were completely polished, Kelly seemed sincere and relatable. Only her powerful, touching voice made her seem out of the ordinary. Watching Kelly transform into a confident, poised performer made fans emotionally invested in her career. But once the show was over, there was no way to know whether viewer votes would translate into CD sales.

Simon has admitted to feeling anxious about the sales of Kelly's first single, called "A Moment Like This." If the song didn't chart, there wouldn't be evidence that *American Idol* could really make stars out of its winners. Would people still take the show seriously? He didn't have to find out: "A Moment Like This" went platinum.

Kelly's stardom lasted well beyond the initial hype surrounding her victory. Her first album, *Thankful*, was released in April 2003. In addition to "A Moment Like This," three hit singles helped bolster the album's popularity. *Thankful* sold more than 4 million copies. Before ten years had passed since Kelly's *Idol* victory, she had three more hit albums to her name, as well as two Grammy Awards and many other honors. The original winner of *American Idol* proved to be a unique success story.

EARLY VENTURES

When Simon Cowell, Simon Fuller, and the Fox network realized what a hit *American Idol* had become, they looked into expanding the brand as much as they could. They worked out **endorsement** deals with new sponsors. In October 2002, they sent the top ten contestants of Season 1 on a 28-city nationwide tour called *American Idols Live!* This tour became the model for subsequent post-seasons, although later tours were held in the summer.

The Season 1 winner and runner-up were contractually obligated to star in a movie produced by Simon Fuller and written by his brother. However, the resulting movie, *From Justin to Kelly*, fared poorly at the box office upon its June 2003 release, and received a critical panning. As Kelly Clarkson confessed to *Time* magazine, "I knew when I read the script [that the movie] was going to be real, real bad, but when I won, I signed that piece of paper and I could not get out of it." This provision was removed from future contracts.

The *American Idol* concert tour showcases the performers after they have appeared on the program. It is another way that *American Idol*'s producers use the show's popularity to bring in money.

By 2003, so many international *Idol* adaptations had been produced that an all-star competition, *World Idol*, was put together. On Christmas day in 2003, *Idol* champions from 11 different countries came to the United Kingdom, singing one song each. Each adaptation also contributed one judge. Representing the United States, Kelly Clarkson sang the Aretha Franklin classic "(You Make Me Feel Like) A Natural Woman." Results were announced on New Year's Day, 2004. Kelly came in second, after Kurt Nilsen of Norway.

4

High Notes and High Ratings

American Idol's first season succeeded beyond any expectations. When the show returned, it had a higher budget and some permanent changes. Co-host Brian Dunkleman did not return for Season 2, making Ryan Seacrest the sole host. Twelve people advanced to the final rounds, up from the previous year's ten. Season 2 premiered on January 21, 2003, and concluded on May 21; future seasons had nearly identical airing schedules.

Season 2 ended in a very close race. Gospel-influenced crooner Ruben Studdard beat Clay Aiken, who did especially well with big-band and light rock songs, by fewer than 200,000 votes out of 24 million cast. (However, Clay's record sales were somewhat higher than Ruben's.) In the wake of Ruben's victory, some of Clay's supporters complained that they'd had trouble casting votes. When they called the phone number set up for Clay's votes, they said they heard busy signals. With so many people calling the same number at once, there was a possibility that some calls could have been dropped.

Although producers stood by the results, they took precautions to avoid line-jamming problems in the future. Starting in Season 3, each

Although Clay Aiken was the runner-up during the second season of *American Idol*, he has had greater post-*Idol* success than the singer who beat him, Ruben Studdard.

of the final two contestants could receive votes through three different phone numbers. That way, if a voter kept getting busy signals from one phone number, he or she could try again with two more. As years passed, phone line overloads became even less of a problem as the use of text messaging grew more widespread.

Season 2 contestant Corey Clark reached the top nine, but was disqualified for not disclosing his arrest record. Later, he claimed to have been romantically involved with Paula during filming. Paula fully denied the accusations. When an internal investigation found no evidence for the claims, the network took Paula's side.

VIVID PERSONALITIES

Season 3 kicked off with the usual footage of some of the more bizarre auditions. In one particularly odd clip, auditioner William Hung sang the Ricky Martin song "She Bangs." His off-key singing and awkward dancing left Paula and Randy struggling not to laugh, until Simon cut him off. But the would-be singer didn't immediately fade back into obscurity. Perhaps because people respected his positive attitude toward being rejected, William Hung gained something of a cult following. He released novelty records, appeared in commercials, and visited the *Idol* set several times.

However, other personalities to emerge from Season 3 were notable for delivering quality performances. Even in audition rounds, Fantasia Barrino stood apart with her weathered yet melodic voice and dramatic stage presence. Randy has called her rendition of "Summertime," a song from the musical *Porgy and Bess*, the best performance in *Idol* history. With Diana DeGarmo, Jasmine Trias, and LaToya London, Fantasia was part of the first all-female top four. Fantasia advanced to the season finale, along with Diana, who earned praise for a mature singing voice that belied her young age. The victory song, called "I Believe," was co-written by Season 1's Tamyra Gray. On the May 26, 2004 finale of Season 3, Fantasia was named the winner. She eventually had a few management disputes with 19 Entertainment, but remained successful. Her first two post-show albums earned a total of eight Grammy nominations.

Another Season 3 contestant, Jennifer Hudson, wasn't on the show too long but went on to a remarkable post-show career. She finished in seventh place, even though the judges had predicted that she'd easily reach the top three. A few years later, however, Jennifer's singing talent helped bring her a different honor. She made her acting debut in the 2006 movie *Dreamgirls*, a musical inspired by the story of the legendary Motown

Jennifer Hudson is another talented singer who has gone on to great success after her *Idol* appearance. She won an Oscar in 2007 for her portrayal of Effie White in *Dreamgirls*.

Fast Fact

Carrie Underwood and Bo Bice released the same debut single, "Inside Your Heaven." For the first time in *Idol* history, both versions of the song hit #1 on Billboard's Hot 100 Single Sales Chart.

group the Supremes. For her portrayal of a singer unfairly thrown out of the band, Jennifer won an Academy Award for Best Supporting Actress—an especially impressive accomplishment for a first-time actor. Since then, Jennifer has continued both acting in movies and singing. Her debut album, released in 2008, won a Grammy Award.

DISCOVERING A COUNTRY SUPERSTAR

As Season 4 went on the air in 2005, *American Idol*'s production team made conscious efforts to add a bit more variety to the show. The age limit for auditioners was raised from 24 to 28. Guest judges from several different genres (everyone from rapper LL Cool J to Gene Simmons of Kiss) joined Randy, Paula, and Simon during audition rounds.

With her sunny yet attitude-filled soprano voice and country twang, Carrie Underwood soon emerged as a Season 4 fan favorite. As Simon had predicted as early as the top 11 week, Carrie cruised to the top two, where she won a decisive victory over Southern rocker Bo Bice on May 25, 2005. Although the judges were confident that Carrie would be successful, they weren't sure what kind of album she should make after winning. If she only sang country, they feared she would have a limited post-show audience. They also weren't sure if the country music culture, which tended to reward musicians who spent years building their careers, would welcome a contest winner. However, 19 Entertainment allowed Carrie to stick with the genre she knew best.

This decision paid off: Carrie's debut album, *Some Hearts*, sold over 7 million copies, and her next two albums also did extremely well. The many awards Carrie has received include five Grammies and two consecutive Academy of Country Music Awards for Entertainer of the Year. Although she has received quite a few honors specific to country music, Carrie has said that the judges weren't off base in suspecting that the country establishment would be wary of *American Idol* winners. Still, as she told *USA Today* in 2010, appearing on the show was the best career move for her:

> [Can] you honestly imagine me spending 20 years singing in bars trying to make it? That doesn't fit me at all. And my family didn't have the money to pay for a demo. So what was I going to do? *Idol* was the door God opened for me, and I took my chances.

VARYING STYLES

In 2006, *American Idol*'s heightened age limit paved the way for Taylor Hicks, who was 28 when he auditioned for Season 5. The blues-influenced, gray-haired crooner might have seemed like an unlikely candidate for mainstream fame. Simon, for one, was skeptical that

Season 4 winner Carrie Underwood has had one of the best post-*Idol* careers. More than 11 million of her albums have been sold in the United States.

Although Taylor Hicks (left) was voted the winner of *American Idol*'s fifth season, rocker Chris Daughtry (below) has been the most successful contestant from that season.

Taylor would advance very far in the competition. However, Taylor's devoted fan base (which called itself the "Soul Patrol") brought him a victory over Katharine McPhee, whose vocal style tended to be more theatrical and pop-oriented. As Simon predicted, Taylor's post-victory releases didn't sell as quickly as those of other champions. Still, Taylor's fans stayed loyal, indicating that *American Idol* viewers weren't necessarily fickle. Along with several other *Idol* alums, he found success in musical theater.

It seemed to be a testament to the quality of Season 5's contestant talent that the entire top 9 landed post-show record deals. In terms of record sales, the most successful

Fast Fact

Season 5 of *American Idol* was the first to be broadcast in high definition. This makes the images on the television screen appear sharper and clearer than standard-definition television.

of the season was fourth-place finisher Chris Daughtry. On the show, Chris reminded people of highly successful post-grunge bands like Matchbox Twenty and Fuel—even when he was singing older country or R&B songs. Soon after the season ended, he formed a band called Daughtry, for which he is the lead singer, guitarist, and head songwriter. The group's self-titled debut album sold more than 3 million copies, and its 2009 follow-up album, *Leave This Town*, also went platinum. As of 2010, out of all *American Idol* alums, only Kelly Clarkson and Carrie Underwood have sold more albums than Chris.

Idols on Broadway

A number of former *American Idol* contestants have left their mark on theater—usually in musicals on or off Broadway, where they can show off their vocal chops. Clay Aiken has been featured in *Spamalot*, based on a movie by the sketch comedy group Monty Python. Ruben Studdard played a lead role in *Ain't Misbehavin'*, a musical revue about jazz great Fats Waller; two of his castmates were Season 2 contestants Trenyce Cobbins and Frenchie Davis. The cast album was nominated for a Grammy Award.

In 2007, Fantasia Barrino earned rave reviews for her lead performance in *The Color Purple*, a musical based on the Alice Walker novel of the same name. From 2008 through 2010, Taylor Hicks appeared in a revival of *Grease* on Broadway and in two national tours. Also appearing in the *Grease* revival was one of Taylor's former *American Idol* Season 5 competitors, Ace Young. Diana DeGarmo has been featured in *Hairspray* and *Hair* (Ace Young also appeared in the latter). For his performance in *Rock of Ages*, a "jukebox musical" of hair metal songs, Season 4 contestant Constantine Maroulis was nominated for a Tony Award in 2009. In August 2010, Jordin Sparks made her Broadway debut in the New York City-set musical *In the Heights*, in a limited engagement.

5

Adam Lambert (left) congratulates Season 8 winner Kris Allen during the finale, May 2009. Kris's victory came as something of a surprise, because Adam had attracted a lot of media attention during the season.

Maintaining the Magic

As *American Idol* entered its sixth season, its producers attempted to make the show even more interactive. One project harnessed the show's popularity to benefit worthwhile causes. Ryan introduced a special episode, "*Idol* Gives Back." With numerous celebrity guests, the contestants and staff encouraged viewers to raise funds for *philanthropic* efforts.

Fans had the chance to determine what the winner of Season 6 would release as his or her debut single. Over 25,000 songwriters submitted their compositions. Once Simon Fuller chose the top 20, fans voted for their favorite. The winning entry, "This Is My Now," was written by Jeff Peabody and Scott Krippayne.

Season 6 featured a contestant whose run was particularly amusing or exasperating, depending on a viewer's perspective. The judges panned many performances by Sanjaya Malakar. Simon even claimed he would leave the show if Sanjaya won. Yet the teenager had supporters. Online communities sprang up, encouraging everyone to vote for

Sanjaya just to annoy the judges and producers. Sanjaya seemed to take the uproar in stride. When he was finally eliminated in seventh place, he cracked jokes.

Ultimately, the Season 6 title fell to two singers who the judges took more seriously. The *beatboxing* Blake Lewis reached the season finale with Jordin Sparks, who was named the winner. Only 17 at the time, Jordin was *American Idol*'s youngest champ. (For Seasons 1–9, people had to be at least 16 to audition.) Although Jordin won praise for performing older show tunes and songbook standards, she expressed interest in a more varied post-show output. Her successful singles have

Idol Gives Back

On March 8, 2007, the first "*Idol* Gives Back" campaign was introduced. Midway through the *American Idol* season, an extra-long episode is dedicated to raising money for humanitarian groups partnering with the show. The singers and judges visit with the people who will be helped, and encourage viewers to donate. Many celebrity guest stars join them.

Most charitable organizations that benefit from "*Idol* Gives Back" are based in the United States. American nonprofits include Children's Health Fund, which helps uninsured children find emergency medical care; and Save the Children, which promotes educational pro-

grams for children in low-income areas. Other funds go to food banks in the Feeding America network.

African charities also partner with "*Idol* Gives Back." In some African countries, mosquito-borne diseases like malaria cause health crises. Through the nonprofit Malaria No More, "*Idol* Gives Back" funds help people obtain bed netting to protect themselves from dangerous mosquito bites.

"*Idol* Gives Back" did not take place in 2009. The American economy was shaky at the time, and the production team did not think it was appropriate to solicit donations from the American public. "*Idol* Gives Back" returned the next year.

After winning *American Idol* in May 2007, Jordin Sparks received an NAACP Image Award in 2008 for "outstanding new artist."

included R&B and dance-pop tracks with a more modern, youthful sound. Jordin didn't abandon her signature theatricality, however. In 2010, she joined the lengthy list of *Idol* alums who can be seen on Broadway.

SUSPICIONS

When the semifinalists of Season 7 were introduced, viewers discovered that several of them weren't new to recording studios or huge crowds. Some of these contestants made it to the top 12. Kristy Lee Cook and Michael Johns had signed unproductive major-label record deals. David Archuleta competed in other national singing contests prior to his *American Idol* appearance; he'd met Kelly Clarkson and other *Idol* alums. Carly Smithson released a low-selling album (under her maiden name, Carly Hennessy) with MCA Records in 2001—when Randy was A&R vice president at MCA. A song on Carly's album also ended up appearing on Kelly Clarkson's debut album.

Some viewers thought it was against the spirit of the show to cast singers who weren't exactly undiscovered. They wondered if the contestants with industry connections had advantages over the less experienced. However, executive producer Nigel Lythgoe said that no amount of past experience barred someone from auditioning, as long as he or she was not signed to a record label or management contract while appearing on the show. Carly, for example, was dropped from MCA in 2002. Thus, she was eligible for *Idol* in 2008.

Executive producer Ken Warwick pointed out to the *New York Times* that stories of contestants getting second chances could be compelling. "Very often, people have been damaged by the music business in the past and they turn up and we kind of restore their faith in it a bit. There probably are a couple in there that have had a go before and been unsuccessful."

Later in Season 7, an odd moment raised different questions. On the top five finalists' performance night, they were slated to sing two Neil Diamond songs each. After the first round of songs, the top five gathered in front of the judges. Paula began critiquing both songs chosen by contestant Jason Castro. She seemed confused when it was pointed out that Jason hadn't performed his second song yet. The next day, Paula spoke on Ryan Seacrest's radio show to explain what had happened. She'd accidentally read from the notes she took during Jason's dress rehearsal. Before this incident, it wasn't widely known that the judges occasionally watched the contestants rehearse. Some fans thought it was unfair of the judges to make premature critical calls.

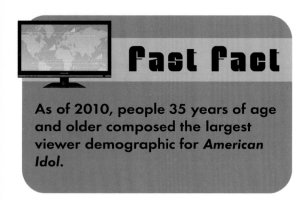

Fast Fact

As of 2010, people 35 years of age and older composed the largest viewer demographic for *American Idol*.

TWO DAVIDS

Controversy aside, Season 7 offered an interesting twist. For the first time, contestants could play instruments on stage. The eventual top two

Simon Cowell did not anticipate David Cook's *Idol* victory. However, David has proven to be a popular performer since winning Season 7. His 2008 album *David Cook* has sold more than a million copies in the United States.

were among the singers who took advantage of this opportunity—former bartender David Cook, who enjoyed adding rock elements to classic pop tunes, played guitar, and high schooler David Archuleta, who specialized in earnest ballads that showed off his vocal range, played the piano.

On the final performance night of the season, Simon proclaimed that Archuleta outperformed Cook in all three songs. Archuleta said he didn't agree with that conclusion. Apparently, neither did viewers, who gave Cook 56 percent of the votes. After the finale, Simon retracted his statements about the final performance night, saying that on review, both contestants had done very well. However, another assessment of Simon's—the prediction that both Davids would go on to forge noteworthy careers—proved accurate. David Cook's self-titled debut album sold 1.3 million copies, somewhat ahead of David Archuleta's 900,000.

Between Seasons 7 and 8, *American Idol* saw some personnel changes. Nigel Lythgoe departed his post as executive producer. And the long-established judging team of Randy, Paula, and Simon would have a new addition, Kara DioGuardi. She'd make her debut on January 13, 2009, when Season 8 premiered.

AN UPSET

Kara might have been new to the judges' panel, but she wasn't afraid to speak up or crack jokes. She also co-wrote "No Boundaries," the Season 8 winner's single. The addition of a fourth judge was exciting, but posed certain problems once the top 12 performance weeks began airing. Performance critiques took longer with four speakers instead of three. A few episodes ran longer than their allotted times. Viewers who used digital recorders were at risk of missing significant moments.

The top two contestants of Season 8 demonstrated that there was more than one successful approach to reaching the *American Idol* finale. A fan of glam rock with experience in musical theater, Adam Lambert brought dramatic flair and a distinctive fashion sense to his flashy performances. Early on, he emerged as a front-runner. Kris Allen, who'd played at bars and coffee houses before auditioning, charmed viewers with minimalist arrangements and quiet but strong vocals. With each solid performance, he gained momentum. Still, so much buzz had surrounded Adam that Kris' ultimate victory came as a big surprise.

After the finale, word spread that fans in Kris' Arkansas hometown had organized parties to build support for him. At the parties, people who didn't know how to send text messages were given help. Some of Adam's voters thought this might have unfairly affected the results. Fox representatives stated confidently that the parties didn't break any rules and weren't unheard of (schoolmates of Carrie Underwood, for example, had held similar gatherings). Moreover, officials from Telescope stated that Kris would still have won without the parties. Nevertheless, such events would be discouraged in the future.

JUDGING SHAKEUP

On August 5, 2009, Paula Abdul announced on her personal Twitter page that she would not be returning to *American Idol*. She said she was very sad to leave, but couldn't reach an agreement with Fox. Her contract had expired, and she did not want to renew it if her salary wasn't raised. Discussions with the network fell through. Randy and Simon said they would miss her, but understood her decision. Nigel Lythgoe called Paula "a special part of the chemistry of the show." However, he added that he didn't think her departure would be damaging. "Of course I believe that 'Idol' is bigger than any one person, and that it will go on. It's been a huge success all over the world with all different judges."

The day before Season 9's January 11, 2010, premiere date, Simon Cowell also confirmed that this season would be his last. His statements didn't indicate any ill will towards the show. Simon simply seemed to feel that it was time to start something new. However, his fans would be able to see him again a year later, when the American version of *The X Factor* was scheduled to launch.

During Season 9's Hollywood rounds, Ellen DeGeneres assumed the seat vacated by Paula. It wasn't her first appearance on the show—in 2007, she co-hosted "*Idol Gives Back*." For years, Ellen had stated that she was a big fan of *American Idol*, and often inter-

Fast Fact

Another longtime member of the *American Idol* staff left the show after Season 9. Music director Rickey Minor stepped down to become the bandleader for *The Tonight Show with Jay Leno*.

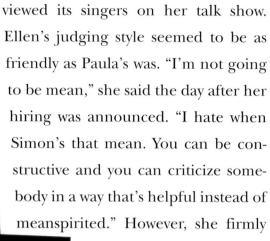

viewed its singers on her talk show. Ellen's judging style seemed to be as friendly as Paula's was. "I'm not going to be mean," she said the day after her hiring was announced. "I hate when Simon's that mean. You can be constructive and you can criticize somebody in a way that's helpful instead of meanspirited." However, she firmly told the press that she wasn't trying to imitate Paula.

CONTINUING LEGACY

Even if *American Idol*'s ratings were declining, the show still had obvious industry clout. Top musicians continued appearing as guest judges and mentors, partly because they realized the value of exposure to such a large audience. For example, Shania Twain saw a 700% increase in album sales

In recent years, many successful recording artists have mentored the contestants on *American Idol*, including Alicia Keys, Harry Connick Jr., and rocker Bono of U2.

after she mentored the Season 9 contestants. An older or relatively obscure piece of music can also get a boost from being played on *American Idol.* After Kris Allen performed a song from the 2007 limited-release musical *Once,* the film's DVD and soundtrack sales surged. When Season 7's Jason Castro performed the Leonard Cohen-penned song "Hallelujah," Jeff Buckley's 1994 version of the song shot to #1 on iTunes. Still, public interest showed signs of a downturn.

Prior to Season 10 auditions, which kicked off in July 2010, producers announced a few alterations to *American Idol.* The producers seemed interested in keeping the show relevant and interesting. Performance nights would run for 90 minutes, so that the contestants' numbers wouldn't have to be shortened, and results nights would be reduced in length to 30 minutes.

In addition, a wider range of contestants would be eligible. Perhaps to attract younger viewers, the show would lower the age limit for participation, enabling 15-year-olds to audition. *Idol* hopefuls also had a new avenue to show off their skills. They could now submit Internet uploads of their songs before auditioning in person.

Time would tell if these tweaks to *American Idol* would increase viewer interest. As Simon Fuller put it, "If the public loses its appetite for *American Idol,* that's fine. Everything has a shelf life." But the show was still ahead of the competition, both in its ratings and in its legacy. As a showcase for new talent and as a game-changer for television, *American Idol* remains unparalleled.

Chronology

2001 On October 5, Simon Cowell and Simon Fuller's *Pop Idol* debuts on the British channel ITV.

2002 *American Idol: The Search for a Superstar* premieres June 11 on Fox; Kelly Clarkson is named the winner on September 4.

2003 Season 2 premieres on January 21, with Ryan Seacrest as the sole host; Ruben Studdard is named the winner on May 21. The *World Idol* performance show is aired on December 25.

2004 Season 3 premieres on January 19; Fantasia Barrino is named the winner on May 26.

2005 Season 4—the first to feature guest judges in audition rounds—premieres on January 18; Carrie Underwood is named the winner on May 25.

2006 Season 5 premieres on January 17. On February 8, Kelly Clarkson becomes the first *American Idol* champion to win a Grammy Award. Taylor Hicks wins Season 5 on May 24.

2007 Season 6 premieres January 16. In February, Jennifer Hudson becomes the first former *Idol* contestant to win an Academy Award. Jordin Sparks wins Season 6 on May 23.

2008 Season 7—the first to allow contestants to play instruments onstage—premieres on January 15; David Cook is named the winner on May 21.

2009 Season 8 premieres on January 13, introducing Kara DioGuardi as a judge. On May 20, Kris Allen is named the winner. On August 5, Paula Abdul confirms that she will not return to *American Idol*.

2010 On January 11, Simon Cowell announces that he will leave *American Idol* after Season 9. The season premieres on January 12; Lee DeWyze is named the winner on May 26.

Glossary

a cappella—without accompaniment from any musical instruments.

beatboxing—using one's voice to imitate the sounds of percussion instruments.

bulimia—an eating disorder characterized by eating excessively (binging), and then intentionally vomiting (purging) what was eaten.

busker—someone who performs in an open, public area and accepts tips from passersby.

choreographer—a professional planner and arranger of dance routines.

endorsement—in advertising, an agreement in which a public figure uses or expresses approval for a product in exchange for compensation from the product's maker.

incumbent—being the current holder of a title or position.

lip-synching—mouthing the words to a song as a recording of the song is played, in order to appear to be singing live.

medley—in music, a number composed of several different pieces that usually follow a similar theme.

montages—sets of short clips that are put together to give an overall impression or tell a story.

novelty—in music, a term that indicates an emphasis on humor or a gimmick rather than long-term artistic value.

persona—the personality that someone presents in public and social settings.

philanthropic—concerned with the well-being of others.

versatility—ability to adapt and function equally well under many different circumstances.

Resources

FURTHER READING

Aiken, Clay, with Allison Glock. *Learning to Sing: Hearing the Music in Your Life.* New York: Random House, 2004.

Archuleta, David. *Chords of Strength: A Memoir of Soul, Song and the Power of Perseverance.* New York: Celebra, 2010.

Barrino, Fantasia. *Life Is Not a Fairy Tale.* New York: Fireside Books, 2005.

Cowell, Simon. *I Don't Mean to Be Rude, But...* New York: Broadway Books, 2003.

Jackson, Randy, with K. C. Baker. *What's Up, Dawg?: How to Become a Superstar in the Music Business.* New York: Hyperion, 2004.

INTERNET RESOURCES

http://www.americanidol.com/

On the official Web site for *American Idol*, fans can find out the latest news about the show and about its current and former contestants.

http://www.19entertainment.com/

The Web site for 19 Entertainment, the production company behind *American Idol* and many former contestants' albums.

http://ellen.warnerbros.com/americanidol/?adid=AI_menu

This section of Ellen DeGeneres's Warner Brothers Web site contains video clips from *Idol* contestants' appearances on her talk show.

http://www.ryanseacrest.com/

Ryan Seacrest's official Web site contains information about *American Idol* and his other media projects.

http://latimesblogs.latimes.com/americanidoltracker/

This *Los Angeles Times* blog recaps *American Idol* episodes and conducts numerous interviews with contestants.

Publisher's Note: The Web sites listed on this page were active at the time of publication. The publisher is not responsible for Web sites that have changed their address or discontinued operation since the date of publication. The publisher reviews and updates the Web sites each time the book is reprinted.

Numbers in **bold italics** refer to captions.

EMMA KOWALSKI is a freelance editor and the author of four books in the MAJOR REALITY SHOWS series. She lives in Nebraska with her husband, Rick, and their two cats, Pepper and Coco.